ANCIENT EGYPT

Stories of Pyramids, Pharaohs, and Discoveries

Samuel C. A.

Ancient Egypt
First edition: agos, 2025

contacto@samueljohnbooks.com

WHAT'S INSIDE?

Introduction 9
Menes: The Unifier of Egypt 13
The Rise of Zoser: The Construction of the First Pyramid . . 21
The Construction of the Great Pyramid of Khufu 29
Hatshepsut: The Queen Who Became Pharaoh 37
Thutmose III: The Empire of the Warrior Pharaoh 45
Tutankhamun: The Boy King 53
Seti I: Warrior and Builder 59
Ramses II: The Great Builder 65
Cleopatra VII: The Last Pharaoh of Egypt 71
Napoleon's Campaign in Egypt 77
Uncovering the Past: The Rosetta Stone and Champollion . . 85
Howard Carter and the Secrets of Tutankhamun's Tomb . . . 93
Final Conclusion 99
Fun Facts About Ancient Egypt 105
Mini Glossary for Young Explorers 109
Timeline of the Great Figures of Ancient Egypt Featured in This Book 113
Questions to Think About or Discuss 117
References 121

INTRODUCTION

Imagine standing in the middle of the desert, beneath a vast blue sky, with the warm rays of the sun shining down on you like golden light. In front of you rise three colossal pyramids, reaching so high they seem to touch the sky. The Great Pyramid of Giza towers above the others, casting a massive shadow big enough to cover an entire village. As you run your hand along its ancient stones, placed there thousands of years ago, a chill runs down your spine. You wonder, "*What secrets do these ancient blocks hold?*" The wind whispers in your ear, as if trying to tell you stories as old as time. Somewhere in the distance, the waters of the Nile reflect the fiery colors of the setting sun.

Egypt is full of mysteries. Every stone has a story.

Here, great monuments still stand—built by powerful pharaohs, rulers who were worshipped like gods. You've arrived in a land where history and mythology are woven together, a place of mighty kings, brave explorers, and unforgettable adventures.

Are you ready to enter this land of wonders and secrets?

Let's begin our thrilling journey through time! But this isn't about learning boring history lessons. No! This is an exciting quest, a series of epic tales where, in each one, you'll live a story filled with action and wonder. Imagine witnessing the discovery of King Tutankhamun's tomb, with treasures glowing in the flickering torchlight before vanishing into darkness. Or imagine the epic reign of Hatshepsut, Egypt's first female pharaoh, who broke tradition and ruled with strength and wisdom.

Each page will transport you to a different time and place, filled with extraordinary events that have shaped Egypt's history. Of course, we can't explore everything—after all, it's hard to fit thousands of years into just one book—but you *will* discover some of the most important moments and characters in this incredible civilization. And through every story, *you* will become part of the adventure.

I bet you already have a favorite hero, right? Well, just like your heroes, the pharaohs and explorers of Ancient Egypt faced great challenges and uncovered amazing secrets that changed the world forever. They braved dangers, solved mysteries, and shaped the course of history. With every chapter, you'll feel like *you're* the one exploring the hidden corners of a lost kingdom or decoding the mysterious writing of a long-forgotten time.

As we uncover the wonders of this ancient civilization, you'll go on adventures that are not only fun but also full of learning. Each story will teach you something important—about courage, about being a great leader, and about how bold ideas can change the world. You'll discover how the ancient Egyptians constructed their awe-inspiring pyramids, established powerful cities, and left a lasting mark on history.

You're about to enter a special kind of classroom—one where every lesson is exciting and every discovery sparks your imagination.

So get ready for a fantastic adventure, full of fun, surprises, and learning! By the time you finish this book, you'll know so much more about one of the most fascinating civilizations in the world: Ancient Egypt. It will feel like you've found a treasure chest filled with knowledge. You'll love it so much, you might even want to keep digging for more mysteries—and who knows? Maybe one day, *you'll* become a great explorer of history!

MENES: THE UNIFIER OF EGYPT

Two kingdoms initially divided Egypt. Uniting them was no easy task—but Menes, also known as Narmer, was determined to make it happen. The regions of Upper and Lower Egypt argued like siblings about who had the best part of the Nile River. Then came Menes with a plan so clever, it will leave you amazed. Ancient artists carved the incredible story of how he united these lands into stone on the Narmer Palette, a powerful symbol of unity and strength that inspired pharaohs throughout history. In this chapter, we'll uncover the symbols and stories told on this ancient artifact.

Get ready to learn how Menes used innovative strategies to turn two rival regions into one mighty kingdom. From important marriages and strong armies to the blending of cultures and the establishment of better government, his brilliant tactics didn't just bring peace—they laid the foundation for thousands of years of Egyptian greatness. Are you ready to discover how the ancient Egyptians became one united people thanks to Menes?

The Narmer Palette: A Symbol of Unity

Long ago, in the land of pyramids and sphinxes, a very special stone was discovered: the Narmer Palette. But this wasn't just any stone—it held the secrets of ancient Egypt and the story of Menes, the legendary figure who united Upper and Lower Egypt into one powerful kingdom.

Carved into its grayish-green surface is the story of how Menes—also known as Narmer—achieved this remarkable feat more than 5,000 years ago. To understand it, we must travel back to around 3100 BCE. Back then, Egypt was divided into two lands—until Menes arrived with a bold plan to unite them, a moment captured forever on the Narmer Palette. The carvings depict Menes as a mighty warrior wearing the crowns of Upper and Lower Egypt, symbols that signify his rule over the entire land as one united entity. The palette is like an ancient photograph capturing the exact moment Egypt became a single nation.

Let's take a closer look at the fascinating images on the Narmer Palette. Imagine this: Menes stands tall and victorious, holding a scepter, while beneath him, mythical creatures called *serpopards* (part snake, part leopard) twist their long necks together. It's an epic scene showing Menes' triumph and the merging of two cultures. And if you look carefully, you'll spot other hidden symbols in these mysterious carvings—like a sacred cow, symbolizing fertility and strength, which were very important during Menes' reign. There's also a mighty bull representing the pharaoh himself, crushing his enemies underfoot. What a thrilling scene.

The Narmer Palette allows us to imagine what life was like during that ancient time—the beginning of Egypt's dynastic period, when pharaohs first began to rule. It was a time of significant change and opportunity. The palette's symbols help us understand how the Egyptians went from being divided to becoming a unified kingdom, leaving behind conflicts to live in peace.

Another remarkable aspect of the Narmer Palette is its lasting influence on Egyptian art long after Menes' time. The pharaohs who came after him saw the powerful images and thought, "I want an awesome crown like that!" The scenes and symbols on the palette became a model for future artists. Its style spread across Egypt—from massive temples to golden jewelry—telling stories of brave kings and heroic victories.

The palette was found in 1897 by British archaeologists in the Temple of Horus at Nekhen. It shows some of the oldest known scenes in Egyptian history, with vivid details of Menes' life and victories. That's why he's remembered as the true founder of a united Egypt. His story didn't end with his death—it lived on through generations, inspiring future rulers to follow his path.

Strategies for Unification

Menes was a very clever leader. He knew that uniting two kingdoms would take more than just strength. He turned to diplomacy and first sought peace through marriage. Menes was from Upper Egypt and married a mysterious woman from Lower Egypt named Neithhotep. He didn't marry her out of love—but as part of a peace agreement between the North and the South. Without swords or threats, Menes used his intelligence to form new alliances and bring the two kingdoms closer together.

But like any great adventure, there were serious challenges. Not everyone wanted a peaceful union. Some people stood against Menes' plans—and that's when our hero proved he was not only a wise ruler, but also a fearless warrior. He built an army and used clever tactics to defeat his enemies. With great skill, he convinced an increasing number of people to join him in his dream of a united Egypt. His courage inspired others, and soon a massive group of allies marched alongside him, all united in their hope for a strong and united land.

But Menes' work didn't end with winning battles. Uniting two kingdoms also meant blending their customs and beliefs. So the great unifier began a new mission: to join the cultures of Upper and Lower Egypt into one. Instead of forcing one way of life on everyone, Menes mixed the traditions, respecting the uniqueness of each region. It was like joining two mighty rivers into one unstoppable stream. This act of respect and inclusion made both people feel like part of something bigger and stronger.

Finally, Menes faced one last challenge: organizing his brand-new kingdom. Picture this new ruler of a

united nation, seated on his throne, studying maps and creating laws to keep peace. With a strategic mind and a heart full of determination, Menes set up systems for taxes, justice, and government to make sure every part of his kingdom ran like clockwork. People saw him as a wise guide, and Egypt became a place of peace and harmony.

And so, Menes—with his bravery, wisdom, and unbreakable spirit—achieved what once seemed impossible: uniting Upper and Lower Egypt not just in name, but in heart. He became a legend, and his kingdom the most powerful of all. The echo of his name still whispers through the sands of time, and his story will be told for generations—as a shining example of how one hero can change the fate of a people, turning two worlds into one: strong and eternal.

Conclusion

The story of Menes, the first pharaoh and unifier of Upper and Lower Egypt, is more than just a tale of crowns and palaces—it's an epic adventure! Thanks to his cleverness, Menes turned rivals into powerful allies. And when things got tough, he used not only strength, but also a mind as sharp as a blade. With brilliant tactics, he led his army like a legendary leader, earning loyalty and respect from all who followed him. In the end, he didn't just create a powerful kingdom—he forged a bond between two once-divided lands.

But Menes' talents went beyond the battlefield. He wisely blended the traditions of both Upper and Lower Egypt, making sure everyone in the kingdom felt respected and included. He always kept this in mind when creating new laws or customs to keep the peace. Due to his actions, Egypt became a mighty nation. Menes was not only a great leader—he left behind a legacy: a united Egypt, filled with peace, culture, and legends that would shine for thousands of years, like the stars in the sky.

THE RISE OF ZOSER: THE CONSTRUCTION OF THE FIRST PYRAMID

Long, long ago, in the blazing sands along the Nile River, there was a pharaoh with an enormous dream. Zoser refused to settle for something as humble as a mastaba when he died—those were the simple tombs built for pharaohs up to that time.

"No!" thought Zoser. "I want to reach the stars!"

And so began his bold plan to build something the world had never seen before: the very first step pyramid!

In this chapter, we'll embark on a fascinating adventure with Pharaoh Zoser and his incredible companion,

Imhotep—possibly the most famous architect in all of ancient Egypt. These two didn't just build something massive with stone—they built a piece of history. Imhotep was a true genius. Architect, priest, and doctor all at once, he brought Zoser's grand dreams to life with his brilliant mind and unstoppable determination.

Now it's your turn to visit that time of construction—where skilled workers pushed their limits, hauling massive stones, and where every broken beam and miscut block became a lesson in learning and perseverance. You'll discover how these two visionaries faced significant challenges and experimented with unknown materials to create something the world had never seen.

Get ready, young historian—your adventure begins now!

The Vision That Transformed Egyptian Architecture

Zoser had a dream as vast as the desert in front of him. But it wasn't just any dream—it was an idea that would stand tall for centuries. Zoser wanted to build something incredible, not just for himself, but for everyone who would come after him —a pyramid.

Before Zoser, pharaohs were buried in mastabas. These were simple, flat, rectangular structures used as tombs. But Zoser imagined something completely different. He dreamed of a tomb that would rise like a giant staircase to the sky. He believed that by building a pyramid, he wouldn't just create a resting place—he would make a symbol of eternal life that would stand the test of time.

But why build something with such a special shape? The answer lies in Zoser's belief in eternity. The ancient Egyptians strongly believed in life after death—a mysterious realm where they would enjoy a second life. Zoser didn't want his tomb to be a simple place hidden under the sand. He wanted it to be a portal that symbolized his rebirth. The Step Pyramid would not only guard his treasures but also protect his life beyond death.

There was just one problem: how could they turn a flat mastaba into a towering pyramid that reached the heavens? It required a massive leap in innovation. Under Zoser's command, architects thought of something new. Instead of the usual mud bricks used up to that point, they chose solid, durable stone. It was a perfect match for Zoser's vision—he wanted to build something that would last forever, something eternal, just like he would be after crossing into the afterlife.

As workers stacked one enormous stone on top of another, the Step Pyramid began to rise. Each layer added more height until it looked like a giant staircase climbing into the sky. People stared in amazement—

they had never seen anything like it before. The majestic pyramid sent a clear message: Zoser was no ordinary man—he was a powerful pharaoh connected to the gods.

Zoser's dream inspired the pharaohs who followed him. They discovered that architecture could be not only functional, but also robust and full of meaning. His bold idea led future rulers to dare build even taller pyramids, such as the Great Pyramids of Giza.

The true power of Zoser's vision wasn't just in the pyramid itself, but in the legacy he left behind. He inspired future leaders to dream bigger, to build grand monuments, to leave their mark on history. Where once there were only simple tombs, now there were glorious pyramids. The shift from mastabas to pyramids wasn't just a change in shape—it was a symbol of power and eternity!

It's incredible to think how the vision of one pharaoh would change the history of architecture forever. Even the great Pharaoh Khufu, who built the Great Pyramid of Giza, was inspired by Zoser. And all of this happened because Zoser dared to imagine something as colossal and eternal as the sky itself.

In the end, the Step Pyramid still stands, an incredible testament to Zoser's dream. It's a historical wonder—and a reminder that when you dream big and dare to do the extraordinary, you can leave a lasting mark. By turning his dream into reality, Zoser secured not only his place in eternity—but also his place in history, inspiring generations to come.

Zoser and Imhotep: Creators of the First Pyramid

Imhotep wasn't just any architect—he was a true genius. Not only an architect, but also a doctor and priest. Together, Zoser and Imhotep accomplished something extraordinary: they built the first pyramid ever—the Step Pyramid of Saqqara! It took great creativity and teamwork to make it happen.

When Zoser decided he wanted something more than a plain mastaba for his tomb, he went to Imhotep and shared his grand dream: to build a structure that would represent his power and eternal life. Imhotep accepted the challenge. With his deep knowledge of geometry and construction, he began planning a brand-new type of building: a step pyramid that would reach the sky.

Their architectural adventure began when Imhotep gathered hundreds of workers, artisans, and builders. Under the burning Egyptian sun, they worked together, sharing ideas and solving problems. The mission was so epic that everyone wanted to be part of it! They devised a clever plan to move the massive stones: they constructed ramps made of mud and earth to slide the blocks into place. It wasn't easy. Beams broke, stones didn't fit, and the desert heat made everything harder. But Imhotep never gave up. He and his team faced every challenge with creativity and persistence. They worked as one, proving that true power lies in teamwork.

At last, the Step Pyramid was complete—ready to defy time—and everyone who saw it was amazed. It wasn't just a tomb. It was a symbol of human brilliance and courage. Even today, people from all over the world come to see it, amazed that Zoser and Imhotep created something so grand without any of the modern tools we have now.

What began as an outstanding achievement became the model for future pyramids. Later pharaohs dreamed of building even greater structures. And who knows? Maybe the famous Pyramids of Giza would never have existed without Zoser and Imhotep! Thanks to them, ancient Egypt was never the same again—and their story teaches us what can be accomplished when imagination and teamwork come together.

Conclusion

Imagine for a moment that you're standing next to Zoser and Imhotep, gazing at their finished masterpiece: the Step Pyramid. Zoser is probably thinking with pride, **"We have built something truly amazing!"** And he's right—because that wasn't just a giant tomb. It was a big idea. A symbol of strength, teamwork, and dreams turned into reality.

They turned ordinary stone into something extraordinary—something that proved what the human mind can achieve. Thanks to this brilliant duo, other pharaohs dared to dream bigger, imagining even more magnificent pyramids. Their story demonstrates the power of collaboration and the importance of never limiting your imagination.

So next time you face something that feels impossible, remember how Zoser and Imhotep made their dream of a great, never-before-seen pyramid come true.

Let their story inspire you to take your first steps toward greatness!

THE CONSTRUCTION OF THE GREAT PYRAMID OF KHUFU

Khufu was the mastermind behind one of the most amazing wonders in the world: the Great Pyramid of Giza! At a time when skyscrapers didn't even exist in anyone's imagination, this pharaoh decided to build something so massive and perfectly designed that it would leave people in awe for thousands of years. His reign was a grand adventure, filled with bold ideas and daring constructions that required more than just strength —they needed great ingenuity.

In this chapter, we'll travel back in time to explore monumental feats and discover what life was like under the rule of this ambitious pharaoh. As you dive into the story, you'll learn how the ancient Egyptians managed to lift those giant stone blocks without cranes or modern machines. But that's not all. You'll also get a glimpse into everyday life during Khufu's time. Imagine a place where everyone—from farmers to artisans—played an essential role in making society work like a well-oiled machine. Religion, teamwork, and a touch of mystery were part of their lives, just like the sun shining over the Nile.

This chapter will immerse you in an exciting mix of history and magical storytelling to help you learn about that time—and have fun while doing it. So get ready for an incredible journey through Khufu's Egypt. You won't want to miss it!

Architectural Wonders of the Great Pyramid

Khufu's name has been carved into history as one of the most remarkable leaders of Ancient Egypt. This great pharaoh left behind a mystery in stone—an architectural wonder that still amazes and puzzles us today: the Great Pyramid of Giza! Get ready for an adventure into the heart of this massive structure, where strength, cleverness, and bravery came together to make the impossible real.

Imagine standing on the sands of Egypt more than 4,500 years ago. Soldiers, workers, architects, and artisans—all gathered to complete a challenge that would stand the test of time. With only simple tools but brilliant minds, Khufu's builders were about to face an epic mission. They invented clever ways to transport huge blocks of stone— some as big as elephants and weighing up to 160,000 pounds (80 tons). Just think of the effort, coordination, and intelligence it took! Stone by stone, these fearless Egyptians raised the pyramid almost to the sky.

Even though we now know they used ramps, historians are still trying to solve the great mystery of exactly how they moved and placed the massive stones.

But that's not all. The Great Pyramid is not just impressive because of its size; it also holds some cosmic secrets. For example, its corners are almost perfectly aligned with the cardinal points—north, south, east, and west—which demonstrates that the ancient Egyptians possessed remarkable knowledge of astronomy. And they did it without any modern instruments!

Standing about 480 feet tall (146 meters), the Great Pyramid was the tallest structure in the world for over 3,800 years. How could this be possible without cranes or modern technology? It remains one of the greatest mysteries of ancient engineering. Experts estimate that between 20,000 and 30,000 workers were needed to build it. These people lived in a special city built just for those who had dedicated their lives to the pyramid. So no, they weren't enslaved, as many used to believe. They were expert builders, skilled artisans, and loyal followers of Khufu, working on a mission to create something that would last forever.

Beyond its enormous size, the pyramid's shape had a sacred meaning. Its pointed top, reaching toward the sky, was like a stairway for the pharaoh to climb into the realm of the gods. The pyramid was much more than a tomb—it was a portal to eternity, built to make sure Khufu could travel safely into the afterlife. This grand tomb represented not only his power on Earth but also his connection to the divine.

The construction of Khufu's pyramid was an endeavor that brought people together from all walks of life, working with a single goal in mind. This incredible achievement reveals how Egyptian society was organized and how, under Khufu's command, everyone worked together to achieve a dream that seemed impossible.

So, the pyramids aren't just piles of stones in the desert. They are symbols of a civilization that dared to dream big—and of a pharaoh who left his mark on history. Today, the Great Pyramid continues to inspire those who look to the past in search of answers. It is a window into another time and a powerful reminder that humans are capable of the impossible.

Daily Life During Khufu's Reign

In Ancient Egypt, life was like a buzzing beehive where everyone had an important role to play. Imagine society as a giant human pyramid. At the very top stood the pharaoh—like the legendary Khufu—ruling over every corner of his vast kingdom. His job wasn't just to wear fancy crowns and lead armies. He had to ensure the entire land ran smoothly, like a perfect machine, where every piece fit together and every life mattered.

Below the pharaoh were the priests, scribes, and nobles. They kept balance in the kingdom, interpreted the gods' messages, and managed the state. Then came the brave and skilled workers—artisans who carved wonders for tombs and temples, and farmers who grew the wheat and barley that fed the nation. These farmers depended on the mighty Nile River, which gifted them rich soil like a sacred present. During the flood season, when the fields rested, many of these hardworking farmers joined in building mighty monuments, such as the majestic pyramids.

Even though this human pyramid might seem like a strict power ladder—with kings at the top and workers at the bottom—each person had an important role to play in keeping Egypt strong. Every group supported and relied on the others, and together they made Egypt shine.

Religion played a significant role in the lives of the people of Ancient Egypt. The Egyptians believed in many gods who watched over everything—crops, homes, even people's hearts. These gods influenced every part of life, from Ra, the mighty sun god sailing across the sky in his golden boat, to Osiris, who welcomed souls into the afterlife. Temples were sacred places where people felt the power of the gods, and where priests performed rituals to maintain *maat*—the cosmic balance—alive.

Imagine waking up in Ancient Egypt at sunrise, with golden sunlight shining on the pyramids, and starting your day with a prayer to Ra, thanking him for his light and warmth. There were no clocks—the sun and the Nile's floods marked the rhythm of life and the passing seasons. Religious festivals were the most awaited events, bringing music, color, and joy to cities and villages.

Art was another essential part of Ancient Egypt. It was a way to keep memories and stories alive. Tomb and temple walls were covered with scenes from daily life, the afterlife, and the glory of the pharaohs. Artists adhered to sacred rules to convey stories both clearly and symbolically. Their job was to create images that would last forever—immortalizing the gods, the kings, and their world.

The Egyptians of Khufu's time were incredibly clever. Even with simple tools and basic technology, they achieved amazing things. Under their rulers' command, simple blocks of stone became eternal monuments—

like the Great Pyramid of Giza, the most magnificent of them all.

Daily life was busy and challenging, but it was full of meaning. People worked hard to build a strong and prosperous society. Artisans sculpted, painted, and built, leaving behind pieces of history so future generations could see their world. Women often cared for their homes, but they could also run businesses and participate in religious ceremonies, demonstrating that their rights were more advanced for their time.

Life along the Nile River was far from boring. Community gatherings, shared meals, and laughter made each day more joyful. And when problems came, the people joined forces, facing challenges with courage and determination.

That was Ancient Egypt—a land where every day was a new adventure. A place of power, wonder, and magic that still echoes through time.

Conclusion

It's incredible to think how the Egyptians lifted those giant stones almost to the sky. The strength and bravery of dedicated workers, who knew they were part of something greater than themselves, made these mighty constructions possible. With their clever minds and determination, they achieved what once seemed impossible.

This outstanding achievement didn't just show Egypt's power—it was a way to challenge time itself, creating something meant to leave future generations speechless.

HATSHEPSUT: THE QUEEN WHO BECAME PHARAOH

The story of Hatshepsut is filled with bravery and thrilling adventures. From her days as a simple queen to becoming one of the most legendary pharaohs of Egypt, her life was full of challenges, discoveries, and heroic feats.

It all began when her husband, Pharaoh Thutmose II, died. Hatshepsut was left as the queen widow, and the rightful heir to the throne was her stepson, Thutmose III, who was still just a young child. At first, she ruled as a regent, which meant she governed in his name until he was old enough to take the crown. But over time, Hatshepsut made a bold decision—

she declared herself Pharaoh. She was no longer just a caretaker of the throne—she was the absolute ruler of Egypt.

Hatshepsut refused to stay hidden behind the palace walls. With fearless determination, she stepped into the world to leave an unforgettable mark in history. She led daring expeditions to distant and mysterious lands, such as Punt, and built astonishing monuments that would last for thousands of years.

In this chapter, we'll sail beside her through uncharted waters to the mythical land of Punt. We'll ride strong ships and uncover exotic treasures in lands beyond imagination. And once the waves calm after this grand sea voyage, we'll step onto solid ground to witness her magnificent building projects—creations so colossal they aren't just made of stone, but are stories carved for eternity.

So get ready, fasten your Egyptian sandals, and open your eyes wide: this chapter will plunge you into a world of daring journeys and majestic monuments—all led by a woman who dared to rule like no one else before her. Through her adventures, we'll discover a tale of ambition and brilliance that will forever inspire brave and curious hearts.

Hatshepsut's Expedition to the Land of Punt

Hatshepsut, the queen who broke all the rules to become Pharaoh, had an adventurous spirit that shone brightly in her most famous mission: the expedition to Punt. This journey became a legendary adventure that proved her courage and her incredible skills as a leader.

Hatshepsut ordered the construction of massive ships, strong enough to cross dangerous and unfamiliar seas. With great determination, she gathered the best sailors, warriors, and artisans, all of whom answered the call of their bold leader. Every part of the voyage was carefully planned—from the food supplies to the captains of each vessel. It was a great challenge, one only an extraordinary leader like Hatshepsut could face. With the wind at their backs and the roar of the sea all around, her fleet sailed toward a mysterious land.

After many weeks of adventure and danger at sea, the expedition finally reached Punt—a land more exotic than anything they had ever seen before their eyes stretched a kingdom of wonders and riches: trees dripping with sweet-smelling myrrh, incense floating in the air, and animals as strange and magical as the Egyptian gods themselves—playful monkeys, graceful panthers, and treasures that looked like they belonged in a fairytale! Hatshepsut's warriors and explorers loaded their ships with these riches, and with the same determination they had set out with, they began the journey home.

When they returned to Egypt, stories of this mythical land and the exotic treasures from Punt amazed the people. The scent of myrrh and incense filled the temples, and the riches brought glory to Hatshepsut's kingdom, making it the envy of all other nations. The trade of valuable goods from that distant land brought not only wealth but also made Egypt more essential and powerful. Thanks to her wise choices and bold alliances, Hatshepsut became a legendary leader—a Pharaoh whose name would be remembered forever.

The expedition to Punt was a trading mission that showed the adventurous spirit of Hatshepsut's reign. Carved into temple walls and told for generations, this story inspired young dreamers and future leaders alike. It proved that a brave woman could conquer far-off lands and leave behind an immortal legacy. Without a doubt, it's a story that makes the imagination soar and awakens the spirit of adventure in every heart.

Her Monumental Building Projects

Among all of Hatshepsut's architectural achievements, one stands above the rest: her magnificent mortuary temple at Deir el-Bahari. A grand sanctuary built at the foot of towering cliffs, where the terraces rose like steps to the sky and the columns seemed to reach for the stars. This temple was her way of showing that the gods had chosen her. For ancient Egyptians, pharaohs were almost divine beings, and Hatshepsut utilized her brilliant mind to demonstrate to the world that she possessed that sacred connection. Her temple was a stunning place, filled with colossal statues and epic scenes carved into the walls, telling of her divine birth and her reign.

Hatshepsut's builders employed innovative building techniques during her rule—methods so advanced that they amazed architects and builders for centuries to come. These ancient masters weren't just building structures—they were creating wonders! With creativity and respect for nature, Hatshepsut and her builders used sandstone and granite to make their buildings as strong as the mountains and as timeless as the Nile. Her ideas inspired generations of builders, and many of those structures still stand today, defying the passage of time.

But Hatshepsut's brilliant mind didn't focus only on temples. She knew that a true leader had to improve the lives of her people. During her reign, she ordered the construction of canals and irrigation systems, enabling farmers to water their crops more effectively—even in times of drought. This system ensured that there was enough food for everyone. She also expanded trade routes, turning Egypt into a powerful center of commerce. Riches from faraway lands flowed into the kingdom, and everyone benefited from the prosperity Hatshepsut brought.

Her temples were more than monuments—they were places of faith and magic, welcoming all who wished to pray and honor the gods. Inside those sacred spaces, the air was filled with the sweet scent of incense, the sound of religious songs echoed, and the colorful murals told stories of gods and mythical beings. The painted walls sparked the imagination of visitors, transporting them to worlds of legends where gods and goddesses battled and joined forces in fantastic adventures. These sacred temples were places where magic and reality blended into one.

Conclusion

Now you know the story of the legendary Hatshepsut—the daring queen who chose to wear the Pharaoh's crown and challenge the limits of the known world. With the heart of an explorer and the courage of a warrior, she sailed to the land of Punt. Just any ruler could not have achieved such a feat, but Hatshepsut, with her unshakable determination, led a fleet across the seas to discover mysterious, far-off lands. When she returned to Egypt, she brought with her exotic treasures that left her people speechless: incredible creatures, perfumes from distant places, and unimaginable riches. Thanks to this, she transformed Egypt into a powerful trade center, where merchants from all corners of the world came to exchange precious goods.

But Hatshepsut's adventure didn't end there. While her caravans crossed routes filled with riches, she worked to leave her mark on history. She ordered the construction of her funerary temple at Deir el-Bahari, a sacred fortress carved into the very cliffs, surrounded by pathways and canals she had designed herself. Hatshepsut also sought to improve the lives of her people. During her rule, she not only built magnificent temples to help them connect with the gods but also made sure there was always enough food and water for everyone. She was the queen of a thousand battles, the master of a thousand projects, making sure that Egypt ran as smoothly as the wind gliding over the desert dunes.

Her reign is a story of courage and power carved in stone—a legacy as solid and eternal as a pyramid.

THUTMOSE III: THE EMPIRE OF THE WARRIOR PHARAOH

Before becoming one of the most powerful pharaohs in Egyptian history, Thutmose III had to wait patiently for his turn to rule. **After the death of Hatshepsut, he finally rose to the throne, and that's when his own spectacular story began.**

Thutmose III was a pharaoh who knew how to accomplish anything he set his mind to—whether in the heat of battle or by leading wisely from the heart of the empire. He wasn't just any pharaoh—he was a true hero of ancient Egypt, with a brilliant strategic mind and the charisma of a great leader. His astonishing military victories and political skills have fascinated historians for centuries, proving that sometimes, the pen can be just as mighty as the sword.

In this chapter, you'll experience thrilling adventures where Thutmose III faces enormous challenges and performs extraordinary feats. You'll witness legendary battles where courage and clever thinking combine to defeat the enemy. You'll learn how marriages didn't just unite families—they brought entire civilizations together! Feel the thunder of chariots racing across distant lands and see how this legendary pharaoh kept the peace with clever messages. As you follow his story, you'll travel alongside Thutmose as he expands Egypt beyond its borders, opening trade routes and uniting cultures—building not just an empire, but a legend that will live forever!

Brilliant Battle Strategies

Imagine standing in ancient Egypt. The sun blazes high in the sky, casting long shadows on the ground. Everything you see, this entire amazing kingdom, is ruled by a very special pharaoh: Thutmose III, the most excellent strategist and warrior Egypt has ever known.

Our first stop on this epic journey is the famous Battle of Megiddo. A massive army of enemy cities had joined forces to face Egypt, hiding behind the strong walls of a fortified town. Thutmose found himself in a tricky situation—but he had a decisive advantage: his knowledge of the land. Instead of attacking the heavily guarded routes, he chose a narrow and mysterious path that everyone believed was impossible for an army to cross. And just like that, out of nowhere, Thutmose's troops appeared and took the enemy by surprise!

In that battle, he proved his ability to predict his enemies' moves. But he also showed he was a remarkable leader—able to adapt and solve problems in the heat of the moment. As chaos erupted, the enemy forces quickly retreated, leaving behind treasures, horses, and chariots. But instead of destroying them, Thutmose III surrounded Megiddo and waited until the leaders inside finally surrendered. He knew that capturing the city without unnecessary bloodshed would earn him a good reputation, showing his fantastic patience and cleverness.

Now, our adventure takes us south, to the rich lands of Nubia—a place full of gold and ivory mines that Egypt needed to grow its wealth. But Thutmose didn't just want their resources; he wanted Nubia to become part of his kingdom. He planned the invasion carefully and, thanks to his skill and support from the local people, Nubia became Egyptian territory.

But Thutmose wasn't just a master of battle plans and politics. He introduced something on the battlefield that changed war forever: **chariots**! Before, most soldiers were foot soldiers. But Thutmose saw the potential of these fast-moving vehicles. Chariots allowed warriors to move quickly, strike, and retreat when needed. The use of chariots gave Thutmose an advantage in every battle—and helped keep Egypt one step ahead of its enemies.

Finally, we arrive at the siege of Kadesh—a city surrounded by strong walls and guarded by fierce warriors. Most people thought it was impossible to conquer. But Thutmose didn't think that way. He believed that with patience and careful planning, he could do it. He kept his troops strong, well-fed, and motivated. They surrounded the city day after day until the defenders finally gave up.

During his reign, Thutmose III led bold campaigns—each more impressive than the last. When all seemed lost, he surprised his enemies at Megiddo and forced them to surrender. He conquered Nubia and won the siege of Kadesh. He showed us that true power doesn't come from brute force, but from intelligence. His story proves that sometimes, the path that seems impossible is the one that leads to greatness.

Building a Mighty Empire with New Allies

Imagine Egypt as a giant game of chess. The pieces? Kings, princesses—even entire nations—moving strategically across the board. One of Thutmose's most brilliant moves was forming new alliances through marriage. Think about it: if you want to be friends with the kid who lives down the street, wouldn't you invite him to your birthday party? Well, Thutmose did something similar. He asked the children of kings to big celebrations at his palace to build relationships—and then arranged for them to marry into his family. That way, he wasn't just uniting people—he was bringing entire nations together! These marriages formed powerful new alliances that made Egypt stronger than ever.

But his cleverness in building an empire didn't stop there. Thutmose knew how important it was to maintain good communication with other rulers, so he sent them written messages on clay tablets to discuss trade, alliances, or to maintain peace. Instead of using swords to solve problems, Thutmose used words. He proved it's better to solve things with a letter than to start an unnecessary war.

But soon, he realized that to make his kingdom truly thrive, conquering land and forming alliances wasn't enough. He needed to expand trade routes. He dreamed of huge markets filled with merchants trading shiny jewels, exotic spices, and treasures from mysterious lands. Back then, trade was like the internet—connecting people from everywhere. Through trade, Thutmose didn't just seek wealth—he aimed to create a mighty, lively empire where everyone wanted to be.

What truly made Thutmose III wise was how

he saw neighboring cultures—not as enemies, but as allies. He looked at other kingdoms as opportunities to build a better empire, not as dangers to be feared. He respected their customs and beliefs and showed himself to be a great leader. By honoring other cultures, he kept peace in the land and avoided conflict. Thutmose built an empire where everyone got along—because they appreciated each other's unique qualities. He wasn't just a mighty warrior—he was a wise leader who made Egypt shine in history as a strong and peaceful land.

Conclusion

And now, we've reached the end of our great adventure with Thutmose III. We've witnessed epic battles, where our hero shone like Egypt's blazing sun. He was, without a doubt, a brave warrior—able to surprise his enemies when all hope seemed lost and win every fight with his mighty war chariots.

But Thutmose wasn't only a fearless warrior. He was also a true master of diplomacy. Through carefully planned alliances and messages of peace, he gained friends and united kingdoms.

His incredible story took us beyond victories on the battlefield and into a world of diplomacy and trade. Thutmose expanded his empire's trade routes, connecting cultures and ideas, building a peaceful and prosperous kingdom.

So, if you ever find yourself ruling an empire one day—remember this: before you choose to fight, try joining forces to build something amazing.

TUTANKHAMUN:
THE BOY KING

Over 3,000 years ago, in a land of towering temples and golden sands, a young ruler rose to the throne—one who would change the course of Egypt's history forever. Get ready to discover the incredible story of *Tutankhamun*, the youngest pharaoh in ancient Egypt! While other children were learning a trade or dreaming of adventures, Tutankhamun had already been given a great mission: to lead a kingdom and guide it with the power of the ancient gods.

In this story, you'll walk the same paths Tutankhamun once walked—through massive temples and bustling marketplaces of Ancient Egypt. You'll witness the rebirth of a forgotten faith. You'll see the young pharaoh restore the worship of sacred gods like Amun-Ra, breathing new life into the grand temples, and meet the wise advisors who helped turn his dreams into a lasting legacy. Get ready for an adventure full of intrigue, treasure-filled temples, and revived traditions. Dare to uncover the legendary story of the boy king!

Return to the Ancient Beliefs

Tutankhamun, Egypt's boy king, was more than just a young ruler—he was a legendary hero who, in his short life, dared to challenge the legacy of his father to restore balance to his kingdom. Though his reign lasted only a few short years—from 1332 to 1323 B.C.—that brief time was enough to begin a new era and return the Egyptian people to the faith in the gods their ancestors had worshipped for centuries.

Before Tutankhamun took the throne, his father—the powerful Akhenaten—had sparked a massive religious conflict in Egypt. Determined to worship only the god Aten, Akhenaten banned the worship of all other gods and destroyed temples that had been sacred for generations. The people were unhappy with this drastic change to their beliefs and felt that Akhenaten was tearing apart the world they knew. But when the pharaoh died, his son—a nine-year-old boy named *Tutankhaten*—was crowned as *Tutankhamun*. With courage and wisdom far beyond his years, the boy king chose to restore balance and bring back Egypt's ancient traditions.

His first significant act was to order the rebuilding of the temples dedicated to the old gods. Sacred places like the temples of Amun-Ra were restored, and once again echoed with prayers, chants, and offerings. These temples, once abandoned and forgotten, were filled once more with faithful worshippers grateful for the return of their beliefs. With this brave act, Tutankhamun helped his people reconnect with their roots and brought peace and order back to the land. The old gods were smiling on Egypt once more.

But Tutankhamun didn't stop there. Under his reign, Egyptian art flourished like never before. Artists were finally free from the strict rules imposed during Akhenaten's time, and they began to create works that celebrated the greatness of the ancient gods and Egypt's mythical history. Temples and palaces were filled with colorful sculptures and paintings that reminded the people of their ancestors' greatness. Thanks to Tutankhamun, the Egyptian people could once again feel proud of their culture—and Egypt returned to its former glory.

Even as a child, Tutankhamun showed remarkable wisdom by surrounding himself with trusted advisors. Among them were Ay, the great vizier, and Horemheb, the powerful general. They helped guide the young pharaoh in making important decisions and taught him all he needed to rule Egypt. By listening to their advice, Tutankhamun ruled with a wisdom that amazed both his people and his enemies. He was not just a boy king—he was a brave leader who united Egypt and restored ancient traditions with peace and harmony.

As time passed, Tutankhamun's fame began to spread. He was seen as a savior who brought back the gods and traditions of Egypt after a time of great turmoil. Stories of the boy king crossed borders, and he would be remembered forever as the young pharaoh who left an unforgettable mark on history.

Many centuries later, in 1922, a British explorer named **Howard Carter** discovered Tutankhamun's hidden tomb in the Valley of the Kings. Inside, he found dazzling treasures—gleaming gold, sparkling jewels, and sacred artifacts that told the story of a pharaoh who had brought greatness back to Egypt. Amulets and statues of the gods revealed a civilization full of magic and mystery. Tutankhamun's tomb wasn't just a place of eternal rest—it was proof of his efforts to bring joy and pride back to his people. But that story—the discovery of Tutankhamun's tomb—is an adventure we will explore more deeply in the final chapter of this book.

Sadly, Tutankhamun died very young. But his name will be remembered forever. With bravery and determination, he restored his people's faith in the old gods and their pride in being Egyptian—something that would live on for centuries. His name became legend, and even today, the world is still amazed by the adventures of the young pharaoh who dared to change destiny and return Egypt to its greatness.

Conclusion

It's time to say farewell to Tutankhamun, as we reflect on the incredible story of the young pharaoh who brought back Egypt's culture, traditions, and religion. We can picture a child who wore a crown that seemed a little too big—but who never hesitated to do what was needed to fix the chaos his father, Akhenaten, had left behind when he tried to worship only one god.

But Tutankhamun brought back the old Egyptian gods and restored the ancient temples. The young ruler listened to his wise advisors, made decisions worthy of a true pharaoh, and revived the art of his ancestors. And though his reign was as brief as a lightning flash in the desert, his story will live on forever in the sands of time.

SETI I:
WARRIOR AND BUILDER

Imagine a leader who could wield a sword as skillfully as he could draw up plans for a temple. A tireless warrior and a brilliant architect. As he rode across the golden sands of Egypt in his war chariot, he was already dreaming up grand buildings in his mind. In this chapter, you'll dive into the thrilling story of Seti I—a leader who could make peace with words and build a temple with a single command. Thanks to his strength in battle, he made Egypt greater than ever, filling it with treasures and glory. He was always one step ahead, and he knew exactly how to face his enemies.

You're about to embark on an epic journey to discover the incredible feats of Seti I, where even the fiercest enemies trembled at the sound of his name—because of his brilliant strategies and his loyal, fearless army.

Get ready to hear tales of hard-fought battles, where dust flew through the air and the pounding of horses' hooves thundered like storms. Soldiers moved like chess masters on a giant board, protecting their mighty pharaoh with precision and skill. And after the battles, we'll explore the glorious temples and majestic monuments he left behind. This is the story of Seti I—an adventure that will leave you breathless!

Seti I's Military Triumphs

Seti I, the mighty pharaoh of Egypt, was more than just a warrior—he was a master of strategy and a fearless protector of his people. In ancient lands full of danger and mystery, Seti fought against mighty armies that charged through the desert in their war chariots, ready to battle for control.

One of the most dangerous places at the time was the city of Kadesh, where the Hittites sought to take power. Seti I was one of the first pharaohs to face them there. With brilliant strategy, he managed to capture the city—at least for a time. Though this battle may not be the most famous, it set the stage for the legendary clash that would come years later, when his son,

Ramses II, would also fight the Hittites in the great Battle of Kadesh. Father and son—one epic struggle, but in different times.

The Hittites were no easy enemy—they were powerful and feared across the land! But Seti didn't just rely on strength. He used clever diplomacy and innovative strategy to take back lands little by little. Thanks to his sharp mind, Egypt didn't just defend its borders—it grew more prosperous and more respected in the ancient world.

But a powerful ruler always has more than one threat. Seti also had to face the Amorites, a brave and strong people who also wanted to expand their power. But Seti, feeling unstoppable, took on the challenge. He knew that true victory wasn't only about fighting—it was about never giving up. The Amorites were tough opponents, but Seti pushed forward with courage. His battle with them teaches us something important: never surrender. With perseverance, you can overcome any obstacle.

The story of Seti is not just about war—it's about leadership, wisdom, and bravery. Only a great leader could organize such victorious armies, plan each move with care, think ahead, and know when to use words instead of weapons. To him, leading was like mastering a great game—where the one who thinks smart and acts brave wins, not the one with the most enormous sword.

So next time you're trying to win at something—

whether it's a game or a challenge—remember Seti. Think of his brave choices and how he used both strength and strategy to protect and grow his kingdom. Seti's story is a treasure for future leaders, showing that with patience, courage, and wise decisions, you can achieve amazing things and chase your dreams!

Seti the Builder: Restorer of Wonders

Seti wasn't just a warrior—he also dedicated his life to building temples and monuments that would change Egypt's history and still amaze travelers today.

He believed that for his kingdom to thrive, the gods had to be honored. That's why he began one of his greatest missions: building the Grand Temple of Abydos—a stunning masterpiece and the crown jewel of his reign. Now, close your eyes and imagine this: rising from the golden desert sands, a massive fortress of white stone. This sacred place was dedicated to Osiris, the god of the afterlife. With this temple, Seti showed the world his deep respect for the gods and his dream of being remembered forever.

But Seti didn't stop at building new temples. He also restored the ancient ones all across Egypt. In doing so, he helped preserve the stories of earlier kings and queens and reminded his people of the importance of remembering their past. When visitors walked through those temples, they could see the beautiful hieroglyphics on the walls and read the old tales of Egypt's history.

Seti's dream of restoring ancient temples teaches us a powerful lesson: we must learn from those who came before us. Every story or carving saved is a piece of wisdom that connects our present to the past. Seti wanted his people to remember their roots and to understand that, to make good choices today, we must know where we came from. Temples were more than buildings—they were places where people gathered, shared ideas, and celebrated their beliefs. They were places of pride, memory, and connection.

Seti's building projects revealed his passion for making Egypt strong and sharing his love for its culture. Temples aren't just made of stone—they are symbols of dreams, beliefs, and identity. His incredible work teaches us that what we build shows who we are. Just like Seti, we can all create something meaningful that lasts. So, next time you start a new project—like finishing a drawing, writing a story, or helping someone—think of it as leaving your mark on the world, just like Seti I did!

Conclusion

We've reached the end of our journey through the time of Seti I, and it's clear: this great pharaoh was not only a fearless warrior—he was a master builder of wonders. He faced fierce enemies in battle and built awe-inspiring temples that have stood for thousands of years.

But Seti's adventure wasn't just about swords and chariots. It's a story of innovative thinking, brave leadership, and leaving a legacy that lasts forever.

Maybe you and I aren't going into battle or building massive temples—but Seti's story reminds us to dream big and be brave. Always remember the wisdom of Seti and dare to bring your ideas to life, combining creativity with strategy. Who knows—maybe one day, your creations will be remembered too.

Until then, let your imagination soar, and always aim for the stars.

RAMSES II: THE GREAT BUILDER

Ramses II was the son of the mighty Pharaoh Seti I—a master warrior and a brilliant builder of temples. From a young age, Ramses traveled with his father and learned from him the secrets of leadership, strategy, and how to leave a mark on history. He dreamed of becoming a great pharaoh… and oh, did he succeed.

He was a bold leader who lived a life full of triumphs, both on the battlefield and beyond. He never sat back waiting for things to happen—no way! Ramses led massive armies and built jaw-dropping monuments that still leave us in awe today.

But in this story, you'll not only discover his incredible talent as a leader—you'll also explore the impressive monuments he left behind as proof of his greatness. Every stone tells a story; every temple is a reminder of his legacy. Get ready, because Ramses II wasn't just a pharaoh... he was a legend whose story still amazes us centuries later. This is an adventure you'll never forget!

The Battle of Kadesh

In the world of ancient Egypt, few names echo as powerfully as Ramses II—famous for his long reign, his mighty temples, and his mastery of war. One of his most epic battles was the Battle of Kadesh—a clash between the Egyptians and the Hittites in what is now modern-day Syria.

Years earlier, his father, Seti I, had fought for this city, capturing it briefly. But the Hittites came back, and the conflict remained unresolved. Now, as the new pharaoh, Ramses II chose to finish what his father had started and set out to face the Hittites, determined to reclaim the region.

What happened next became one of the most legendary battles in all of ancient Egyptian history.

Near the Orontes River, under the burning sun, thousands of fierce warriors faced off. In this great battle, Ramses showed not just his ambition, but also his brilliant military mind. He led his troops into an epic showdown against the Hittites, fully determined to expand Egypt's power.

This wasn't just any battle—it became one of the most significant chariot battles in history, with around **5,000 chariots** clashing from both sides!

But Ramses didn't rely only on numbers—he had a clever plan. While the Hittites used heavy, slow chariots pulled by three horses, Ramses used light, fast chariots that could move quickly and strike with precision. These nimble vehicles gave his soldiers the speed they needed to surprise the enemy and escape before they could be caught.

But then, the unexpected happened. The Egyptian army was caught off guard by a surprise attack. Ramses' soldiers were scattered—and for a moment, it looked like all hope was lost.

Yet Ramses wasn't just any leader. He was a true pharaoh, with the heart of a warrior. Without hesitation, he stayed calm, rallied his men, and launched a powerful counterattack—like a lion charging at its prey. He forced the enemy to retreat and turned the tide of the battle.

In the end, there was no clear victory, nor was there a defeat. It was more of a draw. Still, Ramses didn't see it as a failure. After all, Egypt had not been beaten. When he returned home, he declared it a triumph. He had scenes of the battle carved into the walls of his temples, showing his bravery and strength to inspire his people.

In doing so, he turned that battle into a lasting legend—a tale of courage and strength that made sure his name would shine forever in the history of Egypt.

But beyond victory or defeat, this story teaches us something even more critical: how great leaders act in moments of crisis. Ramses showed that leadership isn't just about giving orders—it's about having the courage to take control, face chaos, and turn it into opportunity. His bravery and clever thinking saved his army and proved that even in the most challenging moments, a true leader can turn the tide.

The story of Ramses II at Kadesh is more than just a lesson in strategy—it's proof that heroes see every challenge as a chance to prove their greatness. Just like Ramses turned a tough battle into a symbol of pride, you too can face your challenges with creativity and determination—and come out stronger on the other side.

The Temples of Abu Simbel

Ramses II's name echoed across the entire kingdom—not only as a fearless warrior, but also as the builder of wonders so amazing they seemed to come from another world. These temples weren't ordinary buildings—they were gigantic sacred monuments that told the story of Ramses and honored the gods!

In those times, Egyptians believed that the gods

chose pharaohs like Ramses to rule the land. So every temple carved from stone was proof that Ramses had the divine right to be pharaoh. When people saw these temples, they remembered the incredible power of their king—and his connection to the gods.

But building these wonders wasn't easy. The ancient Egyptians were master builders. They used tools and techniques so advanced they seemed magical. If you've ever tried stacking toy blocks without letting them fall—imagine doing that with huge stones heavier than an elephant! The Egyptians placed each block with such perfect precision that their temples still stand thousands of years later. Their skills were so incredible that even modern engineers are amazed.

Inside these temples, everything felt magical. Imagine walls glowing with torchlight, priests chanting ancient prayers, and people bringing offerings to honor the gods and their pharaoh. Through these rituals, Egyptians prayed for the Nile to flood on time, for strong crops, and peace to reign. The temples were sacred places where everyone—from the poorest farmer to the richest noble—could connect with the divine. It was a world full of mystery and wonder!

Many centuries later, in the 1960s, people from around the world came together to save history. The temples of Abu Simbel—famous all over the globe—were in danger of being swallowed by water due to the building of a massive dam. But instead of letting them disappear, countries from every continent joined forces to protect these amazing treasures.

With careful planning and teamwork, they cut the temples into giant pieces and moved them to a safer place.

Thanks to this incredible effort, they saved and protected a massive part of history. Moving the temples reminded people everywhere that even the oldest stories are worth saving. And so, the legacy of Ramses II—the great builder pharaoh—lives on today, as an epic adventure that has survived the test of time.

Conclusion

Picture Ramses II standing tall, proud of all he achieved—whether in the chaos of battle or at the front of the towering temples he helped create. Whether he was leading his army at Kadesh or overseeing the massive statues at Abu Simbel, Ramses knew how to leave a mark on history.

With clever thinking and unstoppable courage, he turned near-defeats into legendary victories, while his monuments told the world of his greatness.

The story of Ramses teaches us that with a brilliant plan and the right strategy, almost anything is possible.

CLEOPATRA VII: THE LAST PHARAOH OF EGYPT

Being the Pharaoh of Egypt was never an easy task— especially not for Cleopatra VII. She had to navigate the ancient secrets of the Nile and the dangerous political webs of Rome. But Cleopatra wasn't just a queen covered in beautiful jewels—she was a brilliant strategist, playing with the fate of her kingdom like it was a giant game of chess. With dazzling beauty and unmatched intelligence, she built powerful alliances like someone drawing a treasure map that led straight to the throne. Her cleverness left even the mighty Romans stunned and unsure of what her next move would be. With charm and cunning, Cleopatra broke the rules of the game and got what she wanted. And that's how legends are born.

In this chapter, you'll dive into those incredible times—when Cleopatra, with sharp wit and fearless moves, crossed paths with two of Rome's most famous men: Julius Caesar and Mark Antony. You'll discover how she turned personal relationships into powerful alliances and used her mind like a sword on the battlefield of politics. Get ready for an epic journey through ancient times—and who knows, you might even learn a trick or two for standing out as a leader. Prepare to set sail on a grand adventure and see how Cleopatra shaped her destiny with wisdom, bravery, and a touch of drama.

Cleopatra and Julius Caesar

Long ago, in ancient Egypt, Queen Cleopatra sat by the wide Nile River, her eyes fixed on the horizon, her mind racing with ideas. She had just lost her throne. Her brother, Ptolemy, had cruelly forced her out of the city of Alexandria. Now, without an army or riches, all Cleopatra had left was her sharp mind. But she wasn't just any queen—she was determined to win back her crown.

Far away in Rome, the influential leader Julius Caesar

ruled one of the mightiest empires the world had ever seen. When trouble broke out in Egypt, Caesar decided to go there himself to solve the problem. Known for his military strength and bold plans, Caesar's arrival in Egypt was a golden opportunity for Cleopatra. She had to think fast. She needed to find a way to meet him—and win his trust. With his support, she could reclaim her kingdom.

That's when Cleopatra came up with one of the most famous plans in history: she had herself rolled up in a carpet and secretly delivered to Caesar. This brilliant idea allowed her to reach him without being caught.

Their meeting sparked the beginning of a powerful alliance. Cleopatra knew she had to make a great impression—and with her intelligence and charm, she captured Caesar's attention. That moment changed everything—not just for their relationship, but for the future of Egypt.

Soon, Cleopatra and Caesar grew closer and began working together to solve Egypt's many problems. She wanted to strengthen her reign, and he wanted more power. They shared their plans and helped each other, forming a team that took on the dangerous world of politics. But they couldn't succeed alone—they needed the support of the people. Cleopatra presented her alliance with Caesar as a way to create a better, stronger Egypt for all.

Their bond became so strong that they had a son

together—Ptolemy XV Caesarion, also known as "Little Caesar," a symbol of unity between Egypt and Rome.

But then the story took a dark turn. Julius Caesar was betrayed and assassinated in Rome. When the news reached Cleopatra, she was filled with sorrow and fear. Her protector was gone. Would Rome still stand by her? Or was she now alone?

One thing was sure—Cleopatra would not give up. She knew this wasn't the end, but a new challenge. With courage and clever thinking, she faced every obstacle to protect her son and her kingdom. Her story reminds us that even when the path is hard, strength and determination can lead us to greatness.

Cleopatra and Mark Antony

But Cleopatra's story didn't end there. Her alliance with Mark Antony wasn't just a tale of love—it was a bold decision that would shape the future of two great nations. They both wanted more power and to protect their homelands. Their partnership was part of a daring plan: Cleopatra needed Antony's military support to return Egypt to glory. And he knew that Egypt's treasures could help him win battles.

Yet, back in Rome, their love and power worried their enemies. Octavian, Antony's rival, saw them as a threat to Rome's traditions. This led to the famous

Battle of Actium—a massive sea battle that changed everything. Cleopatra and Antony faced a powerful enemy, and when they lost, Egypt suffered greatly.

Even in defeat, Cleopatra showed immense courage. She stayed by Antony's side until the very end, when both of them died tragically.

Though their ending was sad, Cleopatra's legacy lives on. She was a woman who rose above the odds, using her mind and heart to survive in a world ruled by men. Her life proves that a single person's story can change the course of history. Today, Cleopatra's name still echoes through time. She broke barriers and became more than a queen—she became a legend. And children around the world still hear her tale, learning that even in a world made for kings, a brave queen can leave a mark that lasts forever.

Conclusion

And so we reach the end of Cleopatra's thrilling adventure—one filled with clever plans, brave choices, and dramatic turns. She was a queen who dared to hide in carpets to surprise powerful Romans and win their trust. With her mind and the help of the legendary Julius Caesar, she reclaimed her throne. But when he was betrayed and killed, Cleopatra had to change her plans quickly and never lose hope.

When life gave her another chance through the brave Mark Antony, Cleopatra didn't hesitate. Together, they set off on a daring mission to rule their worlds with wisdom and strength. But after a sea battle crushed their dreams like a storm, Cleopatra faced yet another twist of fate. Still, she never gave up. Our fearless heroine stood tall, showing tremendous courage even when everything seemed lost.

Though her story didn't end in victory, Cleopatra lives on in our memories as the queen who turned her life into an unforgettable legend. A story so powerful, it will be told for generations to come.

Want to learn even more about Cleopatra's fascinating story? Don't miss the book *Cleopatra: The Last Great Queen of Egypt*!

NAPOLEON'S CAMPAIGN IN EGYPT

Napoleon's invasion of Egypt wasn't just about marching soldiers through the desert—it was an exciting quest to uncover secrets hidden for thousands of years. Napoleon led a daring group of explorers made up of scientists, artists, and expert archaeologists. This unusual team set sail for Egypt, armed not with guns and gunpowder, but with pencils, notebooks, and an unquenchable thirst for discovery. They were ready to document everything they found.

This expedition wasn't just to satisfy Napoleon's ambitions—it brought back a mountain of knowledge that amazed all of Europe. In Egypt, they discovered gigantic temples, mysterious hieroglyphs more puzzling than any riddle, and statues that stood like silent giants.

In this chapter, you'll uncover how these brave adventurers brushed the dust off ancient wonders that forever changed the way we study the past. You'll meet the wise men who, wide-eyed and full of passion, recorded Egypt's incredible beauty. You'll travel back to the very moment they made some of the most jaw-dropping discoveries—colossal temples, majestic pyramids, and fascinating artifacts that sparked the birth of Egyptology, the thrilling science of studying ancient Egypt.

You'll also learn the incredible story behind the great book *Description de l'Égypte*, a masterpiece that captured everyone's imagination and became the foundation of Egyptian studies. And, you'll discover a powerful lesson about teamwork and cultural exchange, as these brave explorers worked hand in hand with local Egyptians to uncover long-buried stories of the past.

Let's dive into a world where history and adventure come together, and where the real treasure... is knowledge! A legendary tale that still inspires those who dream of solving the mysteries of the ancient world.

The Role of the "Savants" in Scientific Exploration

In 1798, Napoleon Bonaparte set out on an epic adventure to Egypt—not only with soldiers and weapons, but with an extraordinary team of scientists, artists, and archaeologists. These experts, known as *savants*, were real-life explorers, armed not with swords, but with pens and compasses. Their mission? To uncover the secrets of ancient Egypt, Napoleon made his mark on history in a story that sounds like it came straight from a movie.

Back then, most Europeans knew very little about Egypt. But this team was determined to show the world the wonders hidden in the desert, while also supporting Napoleon's military campaign. Led by the fearless Gaspard Monge, these explorers awakened humanity's curiosity for ancient Egypt. Amazed by everything they saw, they documented every marvel—temples like something out of a storybook, giant pyramids, and mysterious hieroglyphs. Thanks to their passion and hard work, they opened new paths—connecting military conquest with cultural discovery.

A big part of their success came from teamwork. Napoleon's experts worked side by side with the people of Egypt, who shared their knowledge and ancient secrets. Together, they set out on a quest for wisdom. The collaboration between the French and the Egyptians proved something significant: the best way to learn is by sharing and listening. This teamwork led to even greater discoveries and became an example for future adventurers who understood the power of working together across cultures.

Their discoveries helped create an enormous book called *Description de l'Égypte*, where they recorded all the remarkable discoveries they made. This book became a treasure of knowledge, showing the wonders of a civilization that mixed art and science in incredible ways. Even today, it's still one of the most essential works in Egyptology—and a reminder of what you can achieve with curiosity and careful observation.

Back in Europe, stories of the expedition captured everyone's imagination. Children and adults alike were fascinated by tales of faraway lands and ancient mysteries. Napoleon's team of experts inspired people to see curiosity as a way to explore the world. Books and newspapers filled with their adventures sparked a thirst for knowledge in the hearts of children across the continent. Schools began sharing these stories to inspire students, showing how determination and teamwork could accomplish amazing things.

Napoleon's experts didn't just leave us with their discoveries—they also created the foundation for modern archaeology and proved how powerful it is when cultures work together and share their knowledge. With pens and sketchpads instead of rifles and battle maps, these 176 savants proved that the search for knowledge can be the most incredible adventure of all. Their mission reminds us of the importance of protecting history and passing it on to future generations.

The Importance of Napoleon's Expedition in Modern Egyptology

For Napoleon's soldiers and scholars, discovering those incredible wonders for the first time must have been breathtaking. But what Napoleon didn't realize was that this journey wouldn't just change history—it would also mark the beginning of modern Egyptology. His campaign in Egypt sparked a fascination that quickly spread across Europe. People wanted to know more about those mysterious pharaohs, the gods with animal heads, and the secrets buried beneath the desert sands.

Before Napoleon arrived, Egypt was a mysterious and forgotten land to most of the world, its ancient treasures hidden beneath layers of time and sand. But once his team of experts began to dig, they uncovered treasures beyond anyone's wildest dreams. Scientists and adventurers joined the mission, studying ancient artifacts, translating old writings, and piecing together a giant historical puzzle. It was the start of what became known as "Egyptomania"—everyone wanted a piece of that magical history.

Museums across Europe are filled with objects from

Egypt that have left visitors in awe. Imagine walking into a museum back then and seeing a statue of a pharaoh or a scroll covered in strange drawings. It was all brand new and full of mystery. Museums became magical places where kids and adults could travel to distant lands with their imagination.

But the magic of Egypt didn't stay inside museum walls. European buildings began to feature columns and decorations inspired by Egypt's desert temples. Artists painted scenes that made people feel like they were standing by the mighty Nile River. Even fashion adopted mysterious Egyptian styles.

After Napoleon's expedition, the way people explored history changed forever. Before, treasure hunters only wanted shiny objects—they didn't care where they came from or what they meant. All they wanted was gold and riches, even if it meant destroying everything in their path. But thanks to experts like W. M. Flinders Petrie, archaeology became a science. Archaeologists began to dig carefully, take detailed notes, and treat every find as an essential clue to a bigger mystery. They weren't just looking for treasures anymore—they were looking for answers: Who were these people? What did they believe? How did they live?

This new way of studying the past turned excavation sites into giant laboratories. Archaeologists became detectives, uncovering the pieces of an ancient puzzle. With every discovery, the story of ancient Egypt came alive again—allowing all of us to learn about one of the greatest civilizations in human history.

Conclusion

And so ends our thrilling adventure with Napoleon through ancient Egypt. What began as a military mission turned into a quest for hidden knowledge. The fearless savants, armed with curiosity instead of rifles, uncovered wonders that sparked a new passion across Europe to unlock the secrets of the past. Their discoveries weren't forgotten in dusty books—they survived through time and changed how we see history today.

Just imagine how exciting it must have been to explore giant pyramids and try to solve the mystery of the hieroglyphs. Just thinking about it makes you want to be an explorer yourself! These brave adventurers showed us that learning about the past can be one of the most incredible adventures of all.

And their story still lives on—reminding us to keep asking questions, to stay curious, and never to stop learning. Who knows? Maybe one day *you* will be the one to uncover a great secret hidden beneath the sands of the desert.

UNCOVERING THE PAST: THE ROSETTA STONE AND CHAMPOLLION

Cracking the code of ancient Egyptian hieroglyphs was like discovering treasure from another world. In this chapter, you'll dive into an epic mission, where brave men and women tried to solve the secrets hidden within the Rosetta Stone—the key to unlocking a mysterious past. They had to think like great detectives to solve the puzzle of the hieroglyphs. This is the story of how a stone buried in the sand became a legendary object, sparking a grand adventure that led scholars like Jean-François Champollion to unlock the meaning of a forgotten language through courage and determination.

You'll discover how a lucky discovery by soldiers

during Napoleon's campaign in Egypt turned out to be one of the greatest riddles of all time. Meet the fearless explorers who, by piecing together clues from ancient scripts, decoded a new language that revealed a world of forgotten pharaohs, gods, and heroes. Get ready for an adventure through dusty books and shadowy halls full of secrets, and join these heroes on their quest to unlock the secrets of ancient hieroglyphs.

The past is waiting for you!

The Discovery and Importance of the Rosetta Stone

In the year 1799, during Napoleon's grand campaign in Egypt, what was meant to be a regular workday turned into one of the most astonishing discoveries in history. A group of sweaty, sand-covered soldiers was building a fort near the town of Rosetta (now called Rashid). While digging, they found something extraordinary: a large stone covered in mysterious writing. That stone, which would later be named *the Rosetta Stone*, turned out to be a fascinating piece of history—one that, once decoded, would reveal the secrets of ancient Egyptian civilization.

The soldiers didn't know precisely what they had found, but they could feel it was something special. The stone had three different types of writing: Greek, Demotic, and hieroglyphic. This combination was scarce and intriguing, like someone had hidden a riddle just waiting to be solved—a riddle that offered scholars a way to understand a long-lost language.

At the time, no one could read ancient Egyptian hieroglyphs. They were like secret codes carved on walls and objects. But since the Rosetta Stone also had Greek writing—a language many scholars could read—it gave them a unique chance: if they could understand the Greek, they might be able to unlock the other two scripts. It was like finding a map that led to hidden treasure made of knowledge.

At first, few people recognized the stone's actual value. After all, it was just a chunk of rock with writing on it. But as scholars studied it more closely, they realized its incredible power. They were on the verge of solving one of history's greatest mysteries! Step by step, word by word, they began to decode the texts. The process was long and challenging. What seemed like a minor discovery turned into something that would change the world forever.

Over time, the Rosetta Stone became a key piece in the study of Egyptology—the exploration of the language, history, and culture of ancient Egypt. It changed how we see the pharaohs, the pyramids, and the gods of old. Until then, many things about ancient Egypt were still a big mystery. But now, with the Rosetta Stone as their guide, researchers could study the past like never before.

Thanks to this extraordinary stone, we learned that hieroglyphs weren't just pictures, but a complex writing system that represented both sounds and ideas. Without the Rosetta Stone, we might still think of ancient Egyptians as mythical characters instead of real people with lives, traditions, and dreams like ours.

That rock helped us discover who they were, how they lived, and what mattered to them. We learned about their religious ceremonies, their customs, and their daily lives.

Today, the Rosetta Stone is displayed in the British Museum, where visitors from all around the world come to see its ancient inscriptions. It stands as a symbol of the connection between cultures and the human desire to explore the unknown. And even though the stone can't speak, its message is louder than words, telling us the story of a lost civilization—so it will never be forgotten.

Champollion's Great Decoding

Beneath the mysterious sands of ancient Egypt, the Rosetta Stone waited like a hidden treasure—waiting for someone clever enough to unlock its secrets. That person was Jean-François Champollion, a young adventurer from France with a burning passion to understand the enigma of the hieroglyphs. Thanks to his determination, he changed history forever and gave us the key to unlocking the past.

But achieving that goal was anything but easy. Champollion faced a considerable challenge. For years, he studied ancient symbols and strange inscriptions, carefully analyzing each line like clues on a treasure map. To him, every hieroglyph was a piece of a giant puzzle. His effort and dedication teach us that we should never give up in the face of significant challenges.

He wasn't alone in his mission. Like every great adventure, he had allies. Thomas Young, an English scientist, had already discovered some crucial clues. By connecting certain symbols with sounds, he helped Champollion fit together the first pieces of the massive riddle. Sometimes, to solve a great mystery, teamwork is the best tool!

One of Champollion's most significant breakthroughs was realizing that hieroglyphs weren't just pretty drawings—they were part of a secret alphabet. This discovery completely changed the way people saw hieroglyphs. Imagine what it must have felt like to discover that those ancient symbols weren't decorations, but real words in a hidden language, waiting to be read. The Egyptians weren't just carving stories—they were writing sounds, just like we use letters today.

Finally, in September of 1822, the big moment arrived. In Paris, Champollion revealed his discovery to a room full of curious people. The audience held its breath as he explained how he had solved the mystery. Some couldn't believe it. Others were thrilled. But everyone knew they were witnessing a historic achievement.

Champollion's story reminds us that if we follow our dreams with passion and never give up, we can achieve extraordinary things. He showed the world that the most incredible adventure is working hard for what others think is impossible.

Conclusion

Before we say goodbye to this chapter, let's imagine what the world would be like if the Rosetta Stone had never been discovered. We might still believe that hieroglyphs were just scribbles made by someone bored. But thanks to researchers like Champollion, the secrets of an entire civilization were finally revealed.

Through teamwork, curiosity, and brilliant thinking, the mystery of the hieroglyphs was solved—and it became one of the most outstanding achievements in history.

This teaches us that even the smallest discoveries can lead to the most significant breakthroughs. So now, as young explorers, we must remember the story of the Rosetta Stone every time we face a challenge. Please think of the patience, perseverance, and teamwork it took to decode those ancient symbols.

Who knows? Maybe *you* will make an incredible discovery one day.

Keep your eyes wide open and your mind sharp—because just like those soldiers found a mysterious stone in the sand, *you* might stumble upon a hidden treasure when you least expect it.

That might be the most incredible adventure of your life!

HOWARD CARTER AND THE SECRETS OF TUTANKHAMUN'S TOMB

Exploring the secrets of King Tutankhamun's tomb is like stepping into a real-life treasure hunt, full of mysteries and thrilling adventures. Howard Carter and his team braved the burning sands of the desert, determined to uncover wonders hidden beneath centuries of history. Their goal was clear: to find the tomb of Tutankhamun, no matter what. With courage and determination, they ventured into the unknown, ready to reveal the secrets buried deep within the mysterious Valley of the Kings. But like in every great adventure, dangerous trials awaited them, testing their bravery at every turn.

In this final chapter, you'll join Howard Carter

and his fearless companions as they face enormous challenges: floods that nearly destroyed the entire excavation site, and people who didn't believe their mission would ever succeed. You'll witness how, despite the doubts and setbacks, Carter and his team never gave up. Like a true explorer of history, you'll discover that the road to treasure isn't always paved with gold—but with teamwork, effort, and the powerful desire to uncover something truly remarkable.

Get ready for an epic journey filled with obstacles, tests, and amazing triumphs! This is the story of a heroic expedition that led to one of the most significant discoveries in the history of archaeology.

Trouble Finding the Tomb

In the 1920s, Howard Carter and his team lived a real-life adventure while searching for King Tutankhamun's tomb. But their mission was far from easy. Many obstacles stood in their way.

One day, while the team was digging beneath the scorching Egyptian sun, something unexpected happened—dark, stormy clouds suddenly covered the sky. Moments later, heavy rain poured down, turning into a massive storm that flooded everything. Water began rising fast, threatening to ruin all the work they had done. But Howard Carter didn't give up. With the help of his brave team, they quickly covered the most critical areas and dug channels to redirect the water. After a lot of effort, they managed to save the excavation site. That storm not only taught them to respect the power of nature—it reminded them always to be ready for the unexpected.

But that wasn't the only problem they faced. Even though Carter was sure he was close to finding the tomb, other archaeologists didn't believe him. They told him he was wasting his time. Just imagine how hard it must be when no one believes in you—even when you feel deep down that you're about to make history. But Carter wasn't discouraged. Every time someone doubted him, he grew more determined to prove them wrong. And he did. After years of hard work, his team finally discovered mysterious steps carved into the rock. They had found the entrance to Tutankhamun's tomb! It was undeniable proof that Carter had been right all along.

But making that incredible discovery wasn't easy. Working in the Valley of the Kings, under a blazing sun and surrounded by scorching dust, was something only the toughest people could handle. The local workers—skilled and fearless—dug without stopping, shift after shift, despite the heat and sand. They didn't want to waste a single moment in their race to reach the young pharaoh's tomb! This part of the story shows us that archaeology isn't just about finding treasure—it also takes strength, endurance, and a heart that refuses to quit.

Even after finding the tomb, more problems came. When news spread about the treasures hidden inside, Carter and his team had to protect the site from looters. Day and night, they guarded the area with guards and makeshift barriers, making sure no one could enter the place they had worked so hard to find. What was inside wasn't just a bunch of old objects—it was history itself. Carter knew it was his duty to protect these ancient secrets so that future generations could learn about the greatness of Ancient Egypt.

The Treasures of Tutankhamun's Tomb

Inside Tutankhamun's tomb, archaeologist Howard Carter found more than just gold and treasures—he discovered items the young pharaoh used in his daily life. There were tools, board games, and objects Tutankhamun had used as a child. Just imagine the young king having fun with his toys after a long day, or using tools to build things. Even a pharaoh, it turns out, played and enjoyed life—just like kids today.

Among all the treasures Carter uncovered, one stood out above the rest: the legendary **Golden Mask of Tutankhamun**. This mask was a powerful symbol that connected the boy king to the world of the gods. It played a key role in ancient funeral traditions. By placing it over the mummy's face, the Egyptians believed it would protect the pharaoh on his journey to the afterlife. Carefully crafted and full of detail, the mask shows the incredible artistic talent of the Egyptians—and the deep meaning behind their burial customs.

Another amazing object was Tutankhamun's **throne**, shining with precious metals and decorated with powerful symbols that showed the world who ruled Egypt. In ancient times, sitting on that throne meant being the supreme leader—someone who guided their people and earned the respect of all. The throne was a symbol of power, and every detail reminded Egyptians that their pharaoh stood above all others.

But that's not all. The tomb was filled with **mysterious symbols** hiding powerful secrets. One of the most important was the **ankh**, a kind of cross with a loop at the top. For the Egyptians, the ankh was the symbol of eternal life. Anyone who had it was believed to be protected and granted the power to live forever. These symbols weren't just decorations—they were placed there to guard the pharaoh on his journey into the afterlife.

The treasures found in Tutankhamun's tomb show us more than just wealth. They reveal his hopes and beliefs. The ancient Egyptians prepared their kings for an incredible journey—a magical adventure into the next world. Every item found teaches us something about the world of the pharaohs and their gods, where life continued even after death. Exploring Tutankhamun's tomb is like discovering a lost world where the ancient Egyptians live once more, showing us their courage, their faith, and their thirst for adventure.

Conclusion

Just imagine what it must feel like to be the person who dared to chase one of history's greatest treasures, even when everything seemed against him—and to solve a mystery so ancient that it amazed the world for centuries. Howard Carter faced wild storms and a world full of people who didn't believe in him. His story shows us how powerful it is to believe in yourself, even when no one else does. And let's not forget the importance of teamwork. Without his brave workers, Carter would never have found Tutankhamun's tomb. They are the real heroes of this story—facing floods, burning sun, and even dangerous tomb raiders.

When they finally opened the sealed door of the tomb, they discovered more than glittering gold. They learned that Tutankhamun wasn't just a king with great riches—he was a child who laughed, played, and dreamed. History, without a doubt, is like a treasure chest full of hidden wonders, waiting to be uncovered by curious minds like yours.

FINAL CONCLUSION

We've reached the end of our thrilling journey, one that took us soaring over the golden sands of Ancient Egypt, standing beside mighty pharaohs in their triumphs, and joining the quest for mysterious treasures. When you read these last words, turn the final page, and close the book, remember every story as a piece of the giant puzzle that forms the history of Ancient Egypt.

Of course, there are still many more stories we could have explored from this fascinating civilization. If you enjoyed this magical and mysterious world, I encourage you to keep exploring on your own—there's still so much to discover! And who knows? Maybe *you* will be the hero of Egypt's subsequent great historical discovery.

Imagine stepping down from your camel at the end of the desert journey, looking back and remembering all the stops we made. We saw the towering pyramids—not just piles of stones in the sand, but massive monuments built by people so clever that they still amaze the most brilliant architects today. People like Khufu, who didn't settle for building something big—they dreamed of touching the stars.

Along the way, we met legendary rulers like Cleopatra and Tutankhamun. They weren't just sitting on their thrones giving orders. They had dreams and ambitions. They faced real challenges and made choices that changed history forever. You see, history isn't just dates and battles—it's a series of action-packed adventures led by people with dreams bigger than pyramids and ideas sharper than swords.

Even though these mighty kings and queens lived long ago, their stories still capture our imaginations. They were the *influencers* of their time! Their courage, creativity, and determination to achieve greatness are still admired today—and they can inspire you too. So, every time you have a big idea that feels impossible, remember: history shows us that *anyone* can change the world.

As you close this book, don't leave all you've learned behind. Don't think of this as the end. Your adventure doesn't have to stop here. Keep digging into the mysteries of Ancient Egypt—or explore other cultures just as amazing. You can grab another book, watch a cool documentary, or even convince your parents to take you to a museum, where ancient objects are waiting patiently to share their secrets with you.

You don't have to be Howard Carter to make discoveries. You can do it wrapped in a blanket with a book, or while staring at an old object, letting your imagination run wild. Keep dreaming about new adventures. Remember what this journey taught you: the power of being curious, brave, and creative. Do you feel that excitement to explore deep inside you? If so—congratulations! You've got what it takes to become the hero of your adventure. You don't need a crown or an army—just a hunger to learn and a heart full of curiosity.

Every great explorer started as a curious kid who thought the world was magical and full of mysteries. And the best part? *You* are free to choose your path. Your adventure is waiting—whether it's inventing amazing things, writing your own stories, traveling to faraway lands, or simply dreaming big.

One day, *you* could be part of history too. Just remember, you have something many significant figures didn't have: the knowledge of their incredible feats to inspire your own. So go on, fearless explorer—create a story so great it's worthy of being told forever, all around the world.

This may be the last page of our journey through Egypt... but it's also the first page in the story of *your* discoveries. I genuinely hope you've enjoyed the ride, learned many new things, and found inspiration to dream big.

Find your path, because, dear reader, you have exciting stories to live... and wonders to witness.

Now go—*and write your own legend!*

DID YOU ENJOY THESE STORIES?

In the following pages, you'll find bonus content and extra value. But first...

If you found this book interesting or inspiring, please consider leaving a review. It's quick and easy!

It only takes a minute, but it means a lot — it helps more kids and families discover these stories and allows us to keep creating books like this one:

USA UK CA AU

Your opinion is worth gold.
Thank you for your support!

FUN FACTS ABOUT ANCIENT EGYPT

Did you enjoy these stories? Great! Because now it's time to uncover some amazing facts about Ancient Egypt that you probably didn't know. Get ready to be surprised... and to impress your friends!

1. **The Egyptians believed the heart could think!**
   That's right. To them, the heart was the center of thoughts, emotions, and intelligence. They believed the brain wasn't important at all... and they even removed it during mummification!
2. **Cats were sacred animals**
   Egyptians loved cats. They believed cats brought good luck and protected homes. Some gods even had cat heads, like the goddess **Bastet**. Hurting a cat was a serious crime!
3. **Both men and women wore makeup**
   Makeup wasn't just for looks. Egyptians used a kind of eyeliner called *kohl* to protect their eyes from the sun and prevent infections.
4. **The curse of the mummies**
   But not all of them—only the children of nobles and scribes got an education. They learned

to read, write hieroglyphs, and do math on wooden boards or stone slabs.

5. **Children went to school too!**
   But not all of them—only the children of nobles and scribes got an education. They learned to read, write hieroglyphs, and do math on wooden boards or stone slabs.
6. **They had a crocodile-headed god**
   His name was **Sobek**, and he was the god of strength and rivers. Some temples even kept real crocodiles swimming in sacred ponds!
7. **Enslaved people didn't build the pyramids**
   For a long time, people thought enslaved people built the pyramids. But archaeologists have found that they were actually built by well-fed, skilled workers who were respected professionals.
8. **Boats were like floating trucks**
   The Nile River was like a superhighway! Egyptians built boats out of wood and papyrus to carry food, animals, stones, and people up and down the river.
9. **Perfumes came from the land of Punt**
   Remember the mysterious land of Punt, where Hatshepsut sent an expedition? They brought back incense, myrrh, and exotic perfumes for rituals and daily life—and they smelled amazing!

10. **We still haven't discovered all their secrets!** Many temples and tombs are still buried under the desert sand. Archaeologists continue to search for clues, and discoveries are made every year. Who knows? **You** might be the one to find the next immense treasure!

Now that you know all these incredible facts...

Are you ready to become a young archaeologist and keep exploring history?

MINI GLOSSARY FOR YOUNG EXPLORERS

Here you'll find some of the words we used in the stories, and they'll help you better understand the amazing world of Ancient Egypt. Get ready to become a true expert!

Afterlife
The next life Egyptians believed came after death, full of joy, peace, and magical adventures.

Archaeologist
An archaeologist is a person who studies ancient places and objects to learn more about history and past civilizations.

Canopic Jars
Jars used during mummification to store a person's organs. A special god protected each jar.

Cartouche
An oval shape in which the name of a pharaoh was written using hieroglyphs.

Desert
A dry, sandy area with very little water. Much of Egypt is desert, with the Nile running through it.

Dynasty
A group of rulers from the same family. Ancient Egypt had many dynasties over thousands of years.

Expedition
A journey made to explore or discover something new. Pharaohs often sent expeditions to faraway lands.

Hieroglyphs
A writing system that used pictures and symbols instead of letters. Egyptians used them in temples and tombs.

Mummy
A preserved body wrapped in cloth, prepared for the afterlife.

Nile River
The most important river in Egypt. It gave water, food, and transportation to the people.

Obelisk
A tall, four-sided stone pillar with a pointed top, built to honor gods or pharaohs.

Pyramid
A large stone structure with four sides and a pointed top. Built as tombs for pharaohs and nobles.

Pharaoh
The ruler of Ancient Egypt was seen as both a king or queen and a living god.

Sarcophagus
A decorated stone coffin used to hold the mummy of a pharaoh or noble.

Scribe
A person trained to read and write hieroglyphs. Scribes recorded laws, letters, and religious texts.

Statue
A carved figure made of stone, wood, or metal. Egyptians made statues of gods, pharaohs, and animals.

Temple
A special building where Egyptians worshipped their gods and held essential ceremonies.

Tomb
A place where someone was buried. Pharaohs' tombs were filled with treasures for the afterlife.

Treasure
Valuable objects such as gold, jewelry, and statues. Many treasures were placed inside tombs.

Vizier
The pharaoh's principal advisor and helper. The vizier made sure everything in the kingdom ran smoothly.

TIMELINE OF THE GREAT FIGURES OF ANCIENT EGYPT FEATURED IN THIS BOOK

Here's a map through time so you can see when the pharaohs and explorers from this book lived. Now you'll know who came first and how their stories are connected!

c. 3100 BCE – Menes (Narmer)
The first great unifier of Egypt. He turned two rival lands into one powerful kingdom!

c. 2650 BCE – Djoser
Ordered the first stone pyramid to be built—with the help of his genius architect, Imhotep.

c. 2580 BCE – Khufu (Cheops)
Built the Great Pyramid of Giza, one of the Seven Wonders of the Ancient World.

c. 1479 BCE – Hatshepsut
The woman who became a pharaoh. A bold explorer and master builder.

c. 1458 BCE — Thutmose III
The warrior pharaoh. He expanded Egypt's empire and formed powerful alliances.

c. 1332 BCE — Tutankhamun
The boy king who brought back Egypt's old gods and left behind a legendary tomb.

c. 1290 BCE — Seti I
A brave general, great builder, and father of Ramses II.

c. 1279 BCE — Ramses II
A legendary ruler who led the Battle of Kadesh and built the amazing temples of Abu Simbel.

c. 30 BCE — Cleopatra VII
The last pharaoh of Egypt. She challenged Rome and lived a story full of love, power, and tragedy.

1798 CE — Napoleon arrives in Egypt
His expedition included scientists who uncovered ancient temples and the mysterious Rosetta Stone.

1822 CE — Champollion deciphers the Rosetta Stone
Finally, the secrets of hieroglyphs are unlocked. The door to reading Ancient Egypt's past is opened.

1922 CE – The tomb of Tutankhamun is discovered
Archaeologist Howard Carter finds the most famous treasure of Ancient Egypt. The world is amazed!

QUESTIONS TO THINK ABOUT OR DISCUSS

After each adventure, take a moment to reflect, imagine, and share your ideas.

There are no right or wrong answers. What matters is thinking deeply and expressing your opinion.

You can write your answers down, talk about them with someone, or even debate them in class!

Menes: The Unifier of Egypt

- What do you think was harder for Menes: uniting both kingdoms or making them live in peace?
- If you had to bring two groups together that didn't get along, how would you do it?

Djoser: The Builder of the First Pyramid

- Why do you think Djoser wanted to build something so big and different?
- Would you like to be an architect like Imhotep? What would you build?

Khufu: The Great Pyramid of Giza

- Do you think it was fair that so many workers spent their lives building the pyramid?
- What symbol would you build to help people in the future remember your time?

Hatshepsut: The Queen Who Became Pharaoh

- What do you think about a woman becoming pharaoh in a world ruled by men?
- What qualities make someone a good leader, no matter if they're a man or a woman?

Thutmose III: The Warrior Pharaoh

- What would you have done in his place: fight bravely or try to form alliances first?
- Do you think it's possible to conquer without violence? How?

Tutankhamun: The Boy King

- How do you think Tutankhamun felt having to rule as just a child?
- If you were pharaoh at age 9, what would you change in your kingdom?

Seti I: Warrior and Restorer

- What do you think is more important: winning wars or protecting history and culture?
- Why do you think Seti wanted to restore ancient temples?

Ramses II: The Great Builder

- Would you rather be remembered for your buildings or your battles? Why?
- Do you think it's okay to turn a defeat into a story of victory if it helps unite the people?

Cleopatra VII: The Last Pharaoh of Egypt

- Do you think Cleopatra made the right choice in forming alliances with Rome to protect Egypt?
- What would you do if someone unfairly took away your power—would you fight, negotiate, or run away?

REFERENCES

History.COM Editors. (2023, April 24). *Ancient Egypt*. HISTORY; A&E Television Networks. https://www.history.com/topics/ancient-egypt/ancient-egypt

Makyx, B. (2023, August 24). *The Enigma of King Narmer: The Architect of Ancient Egypt's Unification*. Medium. https://bugmakyx.medium.com/the-enigma-of-king-narmer-the-architect-of-ancient-egypts-unification-db9d89280161

Mark, J. (2016, October 13). *Ancient Egyptian Government*. World History Encyclopedia; World History Publishing. https://www.worldhistory.org/Egyptian_Government/

Wilford, J. N. (2002, April 16). *Carving of a King Could Rewrite History*. The New York Times. https://www.nytimes.com/2002/04/16/science/carving-of-a-king-could-rewrite-history.html

Calvert, A. (2016). *Palette of King Narmer*. Khan Academy. https://www.khanacademy.org/humanities/ap-art-history/ancient-mediterranean-ap/ancient-egypt-ap/a/palette-of-king-narmer

Department Of State. The Office of Electronic Information, B. of P. A. (2004, January 1). *Egypt (03/08)*.

2001-2009.State.gov. https://2001-2009.state.gov/r/pa/ei/bgn/5309.htm

Narmer Palette. (2019, September 16). Egypt Tours Portal. https://www.egypttoursportal.com/en-us/narmer-palette/

Ancient Egypt | Lives and Legacies in the Ancient World Class Notes. (2024). Fiveable.me. https://library.fiveable.me/lives-and-legacies-in-the-ancient-world/unit-3

Bowman, A. K., & Dorman, P. F. (2019, January 16). *ancient Egypt*. Encyclopædia Britannica. https://www.britannica.com/place/ancient-Egypt

Egyptian Pyramids - (Origins of Civilization) - Vocab, Definition, Explanations | Fiveable. (2024). Fiveable.me. https://fiveable.me/key-terms/origins-of-civilization/egyptian-pyramids

The Editors of Encyclopedia Britannica. (2018, August 24). *Pyramid | architecture*. Encyclopædia Britannica. https://www.britannica.com/technology/pyramid-architecture

Model of the Temple of Hatshepsut at Deir el-Bahri. (n.d.). The Metropolitan Museum of Art. https://www.metmuseum.org/about-the-met/collection-areas/egyptian-art/dispatches/2012_139_hatshepsut-model

Mark, J. J. (2011, August 1). *Punt*. World History Encyclopedia. https://www.worldhistory.org/punt/

Tyldesley, J. (2018, March 14). *Hatshepsut | Biogra-*

phy, Reign, & Facts. Encyclopædia Britannica. https://www.britannica.com/biography/Hatshepsut

The Editors of Encyclopedia Britannica. (2015, June 19). *Dayr al-Baḥrī | archaeological site, Egypt*. Encyclopædia Britannica. https://www.britannica.com/place/Dayr-al-Bahri

Odler, M. (2017). *Ancient Egyptian Metallurgy*. Press. rebus.community; The Digital Press @ UND. https://press.rebus.community/historyoftech/chapter/ancient-egyptian-metallurgy/

Pbs. (2022, November 15). *King Tutankhamun: Life, Death, & Family*. Pbs; Pbs. https://www.pbs.org/articles/king-tutankhamun-life-death-family

Teeter, E., & Brewer, D. J. (2002). *Religion in the Lives of the Ancient Egyptians*. Fathom.lib.uchicago.edu. https://fathom.lib.uchicago.edu/1/777777190168/

https://www.facebook.com/martina.boshra.b. (2023, September 9). *The Egyptian Museum: A Treasure Trove Of History | EZ TOUR EGYPT*. EZ TOUR EGYPT. https://eztouregypt.com/the-egyptian-museum/

Abydos. (n.d.). World Monuments Fund. https://www.wmf.org/project/abydos

Battle of Kadesh by Ramses II - Battle of Kadesh facts. (n.d.). Egypt Fun Tours. https://egyptfuntours.com/blog/battle-of-kadesh-by-ramses-ii/

Kerrigan, M. (2017, March 21). *Battle of Kadesh |*

Summary. Encyclopædia Britannica. https://www.britannica.com/event/Battle-of-Kadesh

The Temple of Seti I in Abydos. (2023). ARCE. https://arce.org/temple-seti-i-abydos/

Battle of Kadesh: Clash of the Chariot Armies. (n.d.). Warfare History Network. https://warfarehistorynetwork.com/article/battle-of-kadesh-clash-of-the-chariot-armies/

Kerrigan, M. (2017, March 21). *Battle of Kadesh | Summary*. Encyclopædia Britannica. https://www.britannica.com/event/Battle-of-Kadesh

Singh, P. (2023, October 19). *Ramses II, known as Ramses the Great, stands as one of the most….* Medium. https://medium.com/@soamsila/ramses-ii-known-as-ramses-the-great-stands-as-one-of-the-most-68e651001feb

What you need to know about Egypt's Abu Simbel Temple. (n.d.). Bunnik Tours. https://www.bunniktours.com.au/blog/what-you-need-to-know-about-egypt-s-abu-simbel-temple

Contributor, V. (2021, December 20). *The Alliance between Marcus Antoninus and Cleopatra VII | The Roman Empire*. The Roman Empire. https://roman-empire.net/republic/mark-antony-and-cleopatra-alliance/

Editors, H. com. (2019, October 24). *Mark Antony*. HISTORY. https://www.history.com/topics/ancient-rome/mark-antony

Grant, M., & Badian, E. (n.d.). *Mark Antony -*

Alliance with Cleopatra. Encyclopedia Britannica. https://www.britannica.com/biography/Mark-Antony-Roman-triumvir/Alliance-with-Cleopatra

History Extra. (2020, August 21). *Cleopatra, Julius Caesar and Mark Antony: how the last pharaoh's love affairs shaped Ancient Egypt's fate*. HistoryExtra. https://www.historyextra.com/period/ancient-egypt/cleopatra-love-affairs-julius-caesar-mark-antony/

Agai, J. M., & Saragih, M. Y. (2021, July 31). *The Contribution of Napoleon Bonaparte to Egyptology*. Budapest International Research and Critics Institute (BIRCI-Journal): Humanities and Social Sciences. https://doi.org/10.33258/birci.v4i3.2262

Bonaparte in Egypt (2): the scientific expedition. (n.d.). Napoleon.org. https://www.napoleon.org/en/young-historians/napodoc/bonaparte-in-egypt-2-the-scientific-expedition/

Mark, H. W. (n.d.). *Napoleon's Campaign in Egypt and Syria*. World History Encyclopedia. https://www.worldhistory.org/Napoleon%27s_Campaign_in_Egypt_and_Syria/

Napoleon, Egypt and the Birth of Modern Egyptology with Dr. Tara.... (2020, August). The French History Podcast. https://www.thefrenchhistorypodcast.com/napoleon-egypt-and-the-birth-of-modern-egyptology-with-dr-tara-sewell-lasater/

Meier, A. C. (2022, September 26). *Jean-François*

Champollion Deciphers the Rosetta Stone. JSTOR Daily. https://daily.jstor.org/jean-francois-champollion-deciphers-the-rosetta-stone/

Scalf, F. (2023). *The Rosetta Stone: Unlocking the Ancient Egyptian Language*. ARCE. https://arce.org/resource/rosetta-stone-unlocking-ancient-egyptian-language/

Solly, M. (2022, September 27). *Two Hundred Years Ago, the Rosetta Stone Unlocked the Secrets of Ancient Egypt*. Smithsonian Magazine. https://www.smithsonianmag.com/history/rosetta-stone-hieroglyphs-champollion-decipherment-egypt-180980834/

The British Museum. (2017, July 14). *Everything you ever wanted to know about the Rosetta Stone*. The British Museum. https://www.britishmuseum.org/blog/everything-you-ever-wanted-know-about-rosetta-stone

(2024). Sagepub.com. https://cqpress.sagepub.com/cqresearcher/report/download/archaeology-today-cqresrre20020524

Beyond King Tut: An Educational Companion | National Geographic Society. (n.d.). Education.nationalgeographic.org. https://education.nationalgeographic.org/resource/beyond-king-tut/

Mason, E. (2018, July 24). *8 things you (probably) didn't know about Tutankhamun*. History Extra; History Extra. https://www.historyextra.com/period/ancient-egypt/8-things-you-probably-didnt-know-about-tutankhamun/

Wilkinson, T. (2022, December 8). *What King Tut's treasures reveal about daily life in ancient Egypt | Aeon Essays*. Aeon. https://aeon.co/essays/what-king-tuts-treasures-reveal-about-daily-life-in-ancient-egypt

CLEOPATRA: THE LAST GREAT QUEEN OF EGYPT

Scan me

CHRISTOPHER COLUMBUS AND THE JOURNEY THAT CHANGED THE WORLD

Scan me